THE HISTORY OF FOODS
DESSERTS

by Kristine Spanier, MLIS

Ideas for Parents and Teachers

Pogo Books let children practice reading informational text while introducing them to nonfiction features such as headings, labels, sidebars, maps, and diagrams, as well as a table of contents, glossary, and index.

Carefully leveled text with a strong photo match offers early fluent readers the support they need to succeed.

Before Reading

- "Walk" through the book and point out the various nonfiction features. Ask the student what purpose each feature serves.
- Look at the glossary together. Read and discuss the words.

During Reading

- Have the child read the book independently.
- Invite them to list questions that arise from reading.

After Reading

- Discuss the child's questions. Talk about how they might find answers to those questions.
- Prompt the child to think more. Ask: What is your favorite dessert? Do you know when it was invented?

Pogo Books are published by Jump!
3500 American Blvd W, Suite 150
Bloomington, MN 55431
www.jumplibrary.com

Copyright © 2026 Jump!
International copyright reserved in all countries. No part of this book may be reproduced in any form without written permission from the publisher.

Jump! is a division of FlutterBee Education Group.

Library of Congress Cataloging-in-Publication Data

Names: Spanier, Kristine, author.
Title: Desserts / by Kristine Spanier, MLIS.
Description: Minneapolis, MN: Jump!, Inc., [2026]
Series: The history of foods | Includes index.
Audience: Ages 7-10
Identifiers: LCCN 2024058264 (print)
LCCN 2024058265 (ebook)
ISBN 9798892139069 (hardcover)
ISBN 9798892139076 (paperback)
ISBN 9798892139083 (ebook)
Subjects: LCSH: Desserts–History–Juvenile literature.
Inventors–History–Juvenile literature.
Inventions–History–Juvenile literature.
Classification: LCC TX773 .S729 2026 (print)
LCC TX773 (ebook)
DDC 641.86–dc23/eng/20250116
LC record available at https://lccn.loc.gov/2024058264
LC ebook record available at https://lccn.loc.gov/2024058265

Editor: Jenna Gleisner
Designer: Molly Ballanger

Photo Credits: Nubes Studio/Shutterstock, cover; Keith Homan/Shutterstock, 1, 17 (package), 20-21 (cake mix), 23; Chase D'animulls/Shutterstock, 3; THMorningMonday/Shutterstock, 4; Sonja Rachbauer/iStock, 5 (ingredients); chang/iStock, 5 (cake); Bildagentur Zoonar GmbH/Shutterstock, 6-7 (Jell-O); Genesee Pure Food Co. (Le Roy, N.Y.)/MSU Libraries, 6-7 (ad); manyakotic/Adobe Stock, 8-9 (top); ld1976/Adobe Stock, 8-9 (bottom); John Muggenborg/Alamy, 10; Steve Cukrov/Shutterstock, 11 (package); Kristoffer Tripplaar/Adobe Stock, 11 (Twinkies); Ametist_Studio/Shutterstock, 11 (plate); Sheila Fitzgerald/Shutterstock, 12; The Image Party/Shutterstock, 12-13; Neon 2/Interfoto, 14; Plateresca/Shutterstock, 14-15; Shutterstock, 15; Retro AdArchives/Alamy, 16-17; Moving Moment/Shutterstock, 17 (cheesecake); worker/Shutterstock, 18 (left); P. Duff and Sons, Inc. (Pittsburgh, Pa.)/MSU Libraries, 18 (right); RLFE Pix/Alamy, 19; Colleen Michaels/Shutterstock, 20; PeopleImages/iStock, 20-21 (people).

Printed in the United States of America at Corporate Graphics in North Mankato, Minnesota.

This book is dedicated to Britta, Harper, and Sophie.

TABLE OF CONTENTS

CHAPTER 1
Early Recipes 4

CHAPTER 2
Big Brands 10

CHAPTER 3
Mixing Up Cakes 18

QUICK FACTS & TOOLS
Timeline 22
Glossary 23
Index 24
To Learn More 24

CHAPTER 1
EARLY RECIPES

What is your favorite **dessert**? In the early days, desserts were simple. They were made at home. People made them with fruits and nuts. The first U.S. cookbook was printed in 1796. It had two **recipes** for apple pie!

apple pie

It had a recipe for pound cake, too. It called for one pound (0.5 kilograms) each of four **ingredients**. They were flour, butter, sugar, and eggs.

pound cake

CHAPTER 1

In 1822, Peter Cooper learned how to make **gelatin** people could eat. He **patented** it in 1845. Fruit juice and sugar were added. It later became Jell-O! People liked the colors and **flavors**.

> **WHAT DO YOU THINK?**
>
> The first Jell-O flavors were orange, lemon, strawberry, and raspberry. Lime and other flavors were added later. What flavors would you have sold first? Why?

CHAPTER 1

CHAPTER 1

Boston cream pie

Baked Alaska

In the mid-1800s, two new cakes were **invented**. One was Boston cream pie. It is filled with vanilla cream. It has chocolate on top.

Baked Alaska was another. This cake has a layer of ice cream! It is covered in **meringue**.

DID YOU KNOW?

Boston cream pie is named after Boston, Massachusetts. This is where it was invented in 1856. Baked Alaska is named after Alaska. It was created to celebrate the United States's purchase of Alaska in 1867.

CHAPTER 1

CHAPTER 2
BIG BRANDS

Have you eaten a Hostess CupCake? It was created in 1919. The cream filling was added later.

Hostess invented the Twinkie in 1930. It is a **sponge cake**. The creamy filling used to be banana flavored. Now, it is vanilla!

CHAPTER 2   11

In 1935, O.D. McKee made the Oatmeal Creme Pie. It is an oatmeal cookie sandwich. It has creme, or cream, inside. That is how the Little Debbie **brand** started. McKee named it after his granddaughter.

12 CHAPTER 2

CHAPTER 2

In 1938, Ruth Wakefield was making cookies. She added broken pieces of Nestlé chocolate to the dough. She thought they would melt. But they didn't! She had invented the chocolate chip cookie! In 1939, Nestlé bought Wakefield's recipe. They paid her $1. She also got a lifetime supply of chocolate.

Ruth Wakefield

CHAPTER 2

TAKE A LOOK!

What are some of the most popular kinds of cookies? Take a look!

CHOCOLATE CHIP

GINGERSNAP

SNICKERDOODLE

WHITE CHOCOLATE MACADAMIA NUT

PEANUT BUTTER

SANDWICH

OATMEAL RAISIN

FORTUNE

SUGAR

SHORTBREAD

TRIPLE CHOCOLATE

FROSTED

CHAPTER 2

aluminum

16 CHAPTER 2

Charles Lubin owned a **bakery** in Chicago, Illinois. In 1949, he found a way to bake and freeze desserts. He shipped them in **aluminum** pans. Cheesecakes and other desserts could be sold across the country.

WHAT DO YOU THINK?

Lubin named his company Sara Lee after his daughter. What would you name a dessert? Why?

CHAPTER 2 17

CHAPTER 3
MIXING UP CAKES

Do you like cake? Cake mixes make baking a cake easy. In 1930, John D. Duff had extra molasses at his **factory**. He **dehydrated** it. He added flour, sugar, and spices to it. People could just add water and bake fresh cake at home!

Flour companies used this idea. Betty Crocker sold a ginger cake mix in 1947. The next year, Pillsbury sold a chocolate cake mix. In 1951, Duncan Hines sold two flavors. They were vanilla and Devil's Food.

CHAPTER 3

Now, there are many different flavors of cake mixes. They can be made to celebrate a birthday. They can make a regular day special, too! Which is your favorite cake or dessert?

CHAPTER 3

CHAPTER 3

QUICK FACTS & TOOLS

TIMELINE

Take a look at some important dates in the history of desserts!

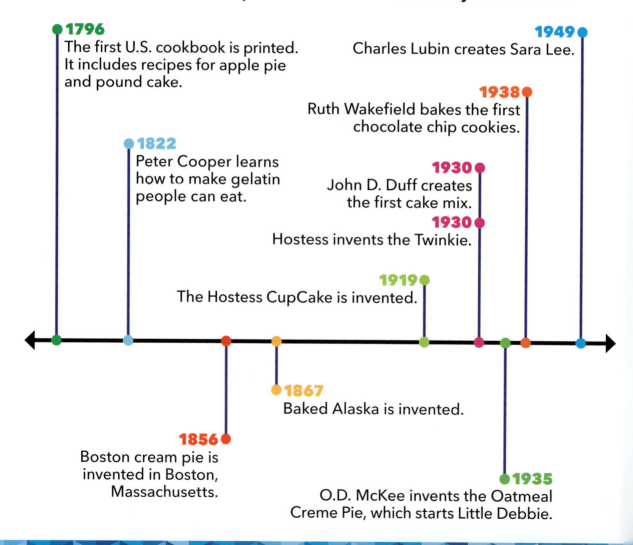

1796 The first U.S. cookbook is printed. It includes recipes for apple pie and pound cake.

1822 Peter Cooper learns how to make gelatin people can eat.

1856 Boston cream pie is invented in Boston, Massachusetts.

1867 Baked Alaska is invented.

1919 The Hostess CupCake is invented.

1930 John D. Duff creates the first cake mix.

1930 Hostess invents the Twinkie.

1935 O.D. McKee invents the Oatmeal Creme Pie, which starts Little Debbie.

1938 Ruth Wakefield bakes the first chocolate chip cookies.

1949 Charles Lubin creates Sara Lee.

GLOSSARY

aluminum: A lightweight, shiny metal that is often used to make cans, foil, and cookware.

bakery: A place where people bake and sell bread, cakes, cookies, and other baked foods.

brand: A name that identifies a product or the company that makes it.

dehydrated: Removed water from.

dessert: A sweet food, such as ice cream or cake, that is usually served at the end of a meal.

factory: A building in which products are made in large numbers, often using machines.

flavors: Tastes.

gelatin: A jelly-like ingredient, made from animal products, that is used to make things like Jell-O or gummy candy.

ingredients: Items used to make something.

invented: Created and produced for the first time.

meringue: A white, fluffy topping made by whipping egg whites and sugar.

patented: Got a legal document that gives the inventor of an item the sole rights to manufacture or sell it.

recipes: Instructions for preparing food, including what ingredients are needed.

sponge cake: A soft, light cake that is made with eggs, sugar, and flour.

QUICK FACTS & TOOLS   23

INDEX

apple pie 4
Baked Alaska 9
Betty Crocker 19
Boston cream pie 9
cake mixes 18, 19, 20
chocolate chip cookie 14, 15
cookie 12, 14, 15
Cooper, Peter 6
Duff, John D. 18
Duncan Hines 19
flavors 6, 11, 19, 20
Hostess 10, 11
Hostess CupCake 10
ingredients 5
Jell-O 6
Little Debbie 12
Lubin, Charles 17
McKee, O.D. 12
Pillsbury 19
pound cake 5
recipes 4, 5, 14
Sara Lee 17
Twinkie 11
Wakefield, Ruth 14

TO LEARN MORE

Finding more information is as easy as 1, 2, 3.

❶ Go to www.factsurfer.com
❷ Enter "desserts" into the search box.
❸ Choose your book to see a list of websites.